A GIFT FOR:

_____

FROM:

_____

DATE:

_____

Crazy About My Wife

Member of the
Evangelical Christian
Publishers Association

PRINTED IN CHINA.

Crazy About Love

LOVE IS PATIENT AND KIND. LOVE IS NOT
JEALOUS OR BOASTFUL OR PROUD OR RUDE.
LOVE DOES NOT DEMAND ITS OWN WAY. LOVE IS
NOT IRRITABLE, AND IT KEEPS NO RECORD OF
WHEN IT HAS BEEN WRONGED. IT IS NEVER GLAD
ABOUT INJUSTICE BUT REJOICES WHENEVER THE
TRUTH WINS OUT. LOVE NEVER GIVES UP, NEVER
LOSES FAITH, IS ALWAYS HOPEFUL, AND
ENDURES THROUGH EVERY CIRCUMSTANCE.
LOVE WILL LAST FOREVER.

1 CORINTHIANS 13:4-8, NLT

I'M CRAZY ABOUT MY WIFE
BECAUSE SHE SAVES ME MONEY
EVERY SINGLE DAY OF THE YEAR!

Honey, you aren't going to believe what was on sale today!

I'M CRAZY ABOUT MY WIFE
BECAUSE SHE ALMOST ALWAYS
SHARES THE COVERS.

(EXCEPT ON THE REAL COLD NIGHTS THAT IS.)

I 'M CRAZY ABOUT MY WIFE BECAUSE
SHE IS ABLE TO SEE BEYOND MY FAULTS.

"Honey, thanks for installing that new light fixture!"

I 'M CRAZY ABOUT MY WIFE BECAUSE
SHE IS ALWAYS READY TO HELP ME
WITH YARD WORK ON A PARTICULARLY
HOT, SUNNY, SUMMER DAY IN AUGUST.

I'M CRAZY ABOUT MY WIFE
BECAUSE SHE HAS MASTERED
THE FINE ART OF MULTI-TASKING.

I'M CRAZY ABOUT MY WIFE
BECAUSE SHE IS FULL OF FRESH
AND CREATIVE IDEAS ON DECORATING
AND KEEPING THE HOUSE
LOOKING NEW.

I'M CRAZY ABOUT MY WIFE BECAUSE
SHE IS A WORLD-CLASS SNUGGLER.

I 'M CRAZY ABOUT MY WIFE BECAUSE
SHE LOVES LONG, ROMANTIC,
CANDLELIT EVENINGS WITH JUST ME.

(AS LONG AS THEY END BY 10:00 OF COURSE!)

I 'M CRAZY ABOUT MY WIFE
BECAUSE SHE STAYS IN SHAPE
AND IS INCREDIBLY DISCIPLINED
WITH HER FITNESS PROGRAM.

I 'M CRAZY ABOUT MY WIFE
BECAUSE SHE KNOWS JUST WHERE
TO TURN WHEN SHE NEEDS A LISTENING
EAR AND A SHOULDER TO CRY ON.

I'M CRAZY ABOUT MY WIFE BECAUSE SHE
DEPENDS ON ME FOR THE MANLY TASKS
AROUND THE HOUSE.

I'M CRAZY ABOUT MY WIFE BECAUSE
SHE TAKES GREAT CARE OF HERSELF
AND IS UP ON ALL THE LATEST
BEAUTY TREATMENTS.

I'M CRAZY ABOUT MY WIFE BECAUSE
SHE KNOWS THERE'S A TIME
WHEN YOU HAVE TO GET TOUGH
WITH THE KIDS.

I'M CRAZY ABOUT MY WIFE BECAUSE
SHE ENCOURAGES ME IN MY LOVE
FOR THE GREAT OUTDOORS.

I'M CRAZY ABOUT MY WIFE
BECAUSE SHE STILL KNOWS HOW
TO GET MY HEART RACING.

No, really, come on in, it's no trouble. I'm glad you stopped by.

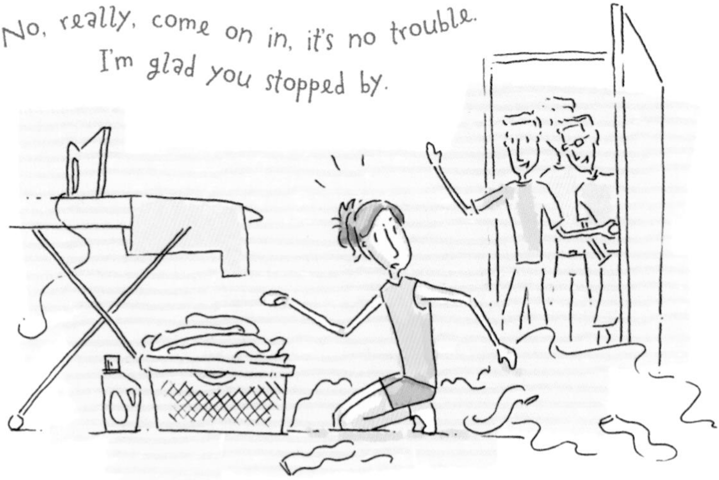

I'M CRAZY ABOUT MY WIFE
BECAUSE SHE'S SO FLEXIBLE.

I'M CRAZY ABOUT MY WIFE
BECAUSE SHE IS MORE RESOURCEFUL
THAN THAT MARTHA WHO IS ON TV.

You made that centerpiece with empty
egg cartons, Styrofoam, and popsicle sticks?

I'M CRAZY ABOUT MY WIFE
BECAUSE SHE BELIEVES IN
TRADITIONAL FAMILY VALUES.

Mom... of course we plan to visit you for summer vacation.

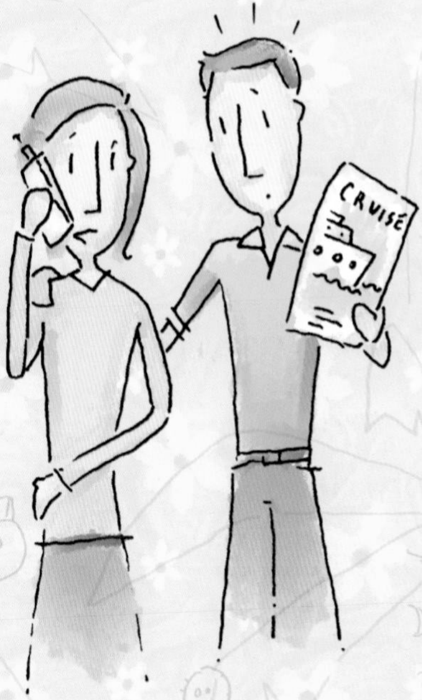

All ri-i-i-i-i-i-ight! Did you SEE that catch?!

I'M CRAZY ABOUT MY WIFE
BECAUSE SHE MAKES AN ATTEMPT
TO SHARE MY PASSION FOR SPORTS.

I'M CRAZY ABOUT MY WIFE
BECAUSE SHE IS
EASY TO SHOP FOR.

I'M CRAZY ABOUT MY WIFE
BECAUSE SHE'S ALWAYS ON TIME.

I'M CRAZY ABOUT MY WIFE
BECAUSE SHE AND I LOVE
WATCHING VIDEOS TOGETHER.

I'M CRAZY ABOUT MY WIFE
BECAUSE SHE REALLY KNOWS HOW
TO GET INTO THE HOLIDAY SPIRIT.

I'M CRAZY ABOUT MY WIFE
BECAUSE SHE KNOWS WHERE
EVERYTHING IS IN THE HOUSE.

Don't forget, we go over to the Smith's
for dinner, and you have a special meeting
at church on Saturday morning, and we have
to send a card to Aunt Lois by Friday...

I'M CRAZY ABOUT MY WIFE
BECAUSE SHE CAN REMEMBER
EVERYTHING WE HAVE TO DO.

I'M CRAZY ABOUT MY WIFE BECAUSE
SHE LOVES CLASSICAL MUSIC
AS MUCH AS I DO.

I'M CRAZY ABOUT MY WIFE
BECAUSE SHE DOES HER PART
TO KEEP ME HEALTHY.

I'M CRAZY ABOUT MY WIFE BECAUSE
SHE DOESN'T ACT HER AGE.

I'M CRAZY ABOUT MY WIFE BECAUSE
SHE CAN WHIP UP A GREAT MEAL
EVEN WHEN WE'RE ALL TIRED
FROM A LONG DAY.

I'M CRAZY ABOUT MY WIFE BECAUSE
SHE BELIEVES THAT CLEANLINESS
IS NEXT TO GODLINESS.

Oh my! And then what did she say?

I'M CRAZY ABOUT MY WIFE
BECAUSE SHE STAYS ON TOP
OF CURRENT EVENTS.

I'M CRAZY ABOUT MY WIFE BECAUSE
SHE IS AN EXCELLENT JOKE TELLER.

So you're SURE you can deliver those flowers within the next hour?

I'M CRAZY ABOUT MY WIFE
BECAUSE SHE NEVER FORGETS
SPECIAL OCCASIONS.

I'M CRAZY ABOUT MY WIFE BECAUSE
SHE KNOWS I NEED MY BEAUTY SLEEP
ON SATURDAY MORNINGS.

I'M CRAZY ABOUT MY WIFE
BECAUSE SHE HELPS ME KEEP
IMPORTANT APPOINTMENTS.

I'M CRAZY ABOUT MY WIFE
BECAUSE SHE IS THE WOMAN
I WANT TO GROW OLD WITH.

I'M CRAZY ABOUT MY WIFE
BECAUSE SHE FOCUSES
ON MY STRENGTHS.

I'M CRAZY ABOUT MY WIFE
BECAUSE I STILL BELIEVE
SHE IS A GIFT FROM GOD.

I'M CRAZY ABOUT MY WIFE
BECAUSE SHE'S STILL THE
ABSOLUTELY ONLY ONE FOR ME.

I'M CRAZY ABOUT MY WIFE BECAUSE
SHE HAS THAT SPECIAL SCENT
THAT CAN MAKE ME
FOLLOW HER ANYWHERE.

I'M CRAZY ABOUT MY WIFE BECAUSE
SHE'S GOT A WONDERFUL WAY
OF MAKING UP AFTER A FIGHT.

I'M CRAZY ABOUT MY WIFE
BECAUSE OF THOSE INCREDIBLE EYES
THAT STILL MELT MY HEART.

I'M CRAZY ABOUT MY WIFE
BECAUSE WITH HER NEXT TO ME,
I ALWAYS LOOK GOOD!

I'M CRAZY ABOUT MY WIFE BECAUSE
SHE KNOWS HOW TO CHEER ME UP
AFTER A TOUGH DAY!

You wouldn't get mad if I gave you a back rub, would you?

I'M CRAZY ABOUT MY WIFE
BECAUSE SHE REALLY DOES KNOW
WHERE TO TURN FOR HELP.

I'M CRAZY ABOUT MY WIFE BECAUSE SHE'S STILL THE ONLY ONE FOR ME!

EVERY TIME I THINK OF YOU, I GIVE THANKS TO MY GOD. I ALWAYS PRAY FOR YOU, AND I MAKE MY REQUESTS WITH A HEART FULL OF JOY.

PHILIPPIANS 1:3-4, NLT